DAGGERS DRAWN

daggersdrawn.net

Published by
Chatsworth Press
P.O. Box 3628
Glyndon, Maryland
21071
kaltoons.com

Design
Glenn Dellon / Dellon Design
529 North Charles Street 101
Baltimore, Maryland
21201
gdellon@comcast.net

Editor
M. William Salganik

Printing
Schmitz Press
37 Loveton Circle
Sparks, Maryland
21152
schmitzpress.com

All cartoons in this book are from The Economist.
©1978-2013

ISBN — 978-1-4675-6818-0
Library of Congress Control Number: 2013934621

Kevin Kallaugher's cartoons are distributed exclusively by
CartoonArts International / The New York Times Syndicate
67 Riverside Drive
New York, New York
10024
nytsyn.com/cartoons

DAGGERS DRAWN

35 Years of Kal Cartoons in

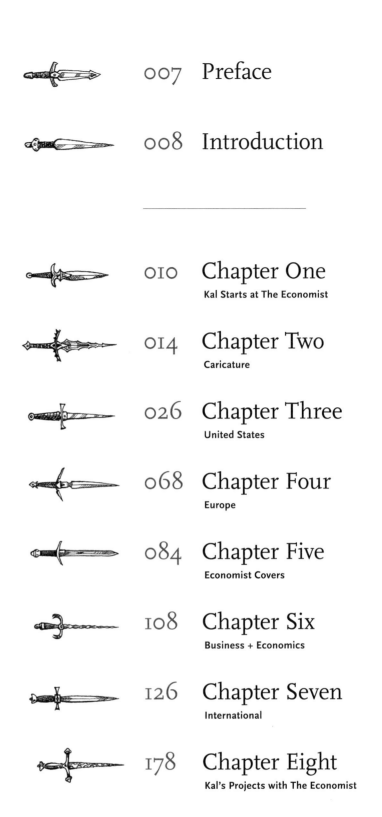

007 Preface

008 Introduction

010 Chapter One
Kal Starts at The Economist

014 Chapter Two
Caricature

026 Chapter Three
United States

068 Chapter Four
Europe

084 Chapter Five
Economist Covers

108 Chapter Six
Business + Economics

126 Chapter Seven
International

178 Chapter Eight
Kal's Projects with The Economist

189 About

190 Acknowledgements

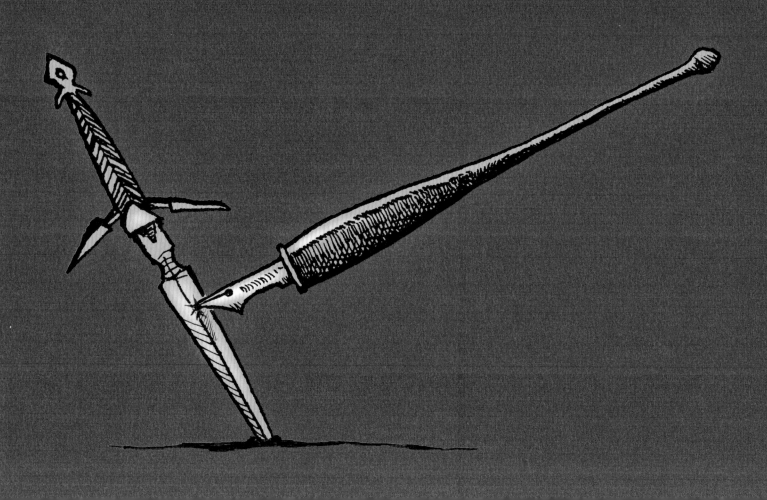

Preface

I have been drawing since I was six years old. I think the six-year-old me would be pretty impressed with this book. It has lots of funny drawings, many of them in colour, and even has a board game (see page 181).

But I think the little kid in me would be particularly amazed at how this book was published.

When my 35th anniversary with The Economist was approaching, I decided to issue a special collection of my Economist cartoons and covers. To make this happen, I figured I needed about $20,000 to produce a modest-sized collection. I opted to employ the newest method to raise capital for projects like mine: crowdfunding.

I turned to the crowdfunding website Kickstarter.com for help. I needed to make a pitch for my project, create a promotional video, and establish levels of giving for backers to join the Kal team. To entice backers I offered goodies such as copies of the new book, cartoon and cover artwork, or prints. I had 30 days to raise the money.

The response was overwhelming. When the month-long campaign concluded, the Daggers Drawn project had raised $100,219 from 1,462 backers. Now instead of the modest book originally planned, the additional funds have allowed me to publish this hefty publication you hold in your hands – more colour, more and bigger pages.

I am incredibly grateful for the tremendous support of the Kickstarter backers, all of whose name are listed in the book starting on page 191.

While assembling the book I spent months trying to locate the thousands of cartoons and covers that I produced for The Economist. Every week I have been discovering new forgotten illustrations. Unfortunately, even with the largesse of my Kickstarter backers there are not enough pages to fit all the cartoons I wanted to publish. That's a shame.

Still, assembling this book has been an incredibly rewarding experience. Re-examining my career as an artist has been gratifying, and the great support during the fundraising was humbling. I hope you enjoy the final product as much as I think the six-year-old me would have.

Lincoln at Gettysburg,
Fitch Elemenatary School,
Norwalk, CT
1961

Introduction

Margaret Thatcher, in one of her unintended moments of humour, once proclaimed that "every prime minister needs a Willie." (She was referring to Willie Whitelaw, her long-standing, loyal deputy). Every Economist editor needs a Kal.

For all the concentration on words at The Economist, nothing unhinges an editor's mind more than a cover subject that seems impossible to illustrate. Sometimes, the pain and panic mount gradually. One particularly hellish example was hell itself, our Christmas cover in 2012. For several months I was convinced that an idea would appear, something funny and poignant. But nothing did. Until in the depths of December, the obvious answer appeared: call Kal (see page 106). In other cases, the drama is rapid. With the showdown in Florida between George W. Bush and Al Gore in November 2000, there was no time, the result was unclear, panic was setting in. Until, of course, my predecessor called Kal (see page 39).

So many of your nightmares are answered by a moustachioed man from Baltimore that there should really be a red button under the editor's desk. The point about Kal, from an editor's point of view, is not just that he saves your skin. He does so with such exquisite politeness and calm that you forget that you were ever in trouble in the first place. There is no subject that defeats him or unnerves him. As Kevin removes the problem from your hands, you feel reason beginning to seep back into other parts of your decision-making process. Your panic disappears.

Kal soothes your brow in other ways too. Every editor has the odd bad week. It is Friday morning and you are still worried that the issue did not go well: maybe we were wrong about Syria? Should we have got that story about Angela Merkel into the paper? And then, as you flick through, your eye catches the Lexington column or the editorial cartoon, and you find yourself smiling, because Kal has come up with something ingenious, pointed and amusing. You become a reader.

And that is the real way to appreciate both Kal and this wonderful book. Nowadays cartoonists are an endangered breed. That is sadly physically true in too many parts of the world: nothing enrages a tyrant more than a caricature (see page 152). But it is also true in places where the rich and powerful have less dramatic means of redress. Across America, editorial cartoonists have been shed: they are too difficult, too pesky, a luxury. Or so some people think.

This book shows how wrong they are. Nobody would accuse The Economist of undervaluing the power of the written word. Yet in drawing after drawing, you will find cartoons that are indeed worth the proverbial thousand words. The daggers, once drawn, are used with rapier-like expertise.

Cartoonists, to make a wildly inaccurate generalisation, tend either to be funny or good at drawing. The beauty of Kevin is that he can do both. The draughtsmanship is exquisite: you always know who the subject of a Kal cartoon is. In some cases you start to get confused between the Kal and the real thing: Bill Clinton's chin seems strangely smaller in the flesh, Tony Blair's toothy grin seems somewhat toothless. And yet there is always a point, a story and a joke with Kal. And there is often a smile. It is the small things that make me laugh most, like a "How's my invading?" bumper sticker on the American tank in Iraq (see page 131) or the dragon in Kim Jong Il's hair (see page 21). Some are worryingly prophetic, such as his cartoon in 1997 (see page 70) of European Monetary Union: the train hurtling round the corner, the track still unbuilt.

Is there anything wrong with this paragon of modern journalism? Yes, his spelling. I think he may have found six different ways to spell Afghanistan alone. Cartoons with lots of words, like the one on page 127, start my heart racing. But this time, the tables are turned, and seeing that Kevin is my editor, it will be his reponsibility this time, but I know I will be in extremly safe hans.

John Micklethwait
Editor-in-Chief, The Economist
MARCH 2013

William Whitelaw,
Conservative Party politician
17 July, 1982

The Economist

1

The Economist Building
25 St James's Street
London SW1A 1HG
telephone: 01-930 5155
telex: 24344
telegrams and cables:
Mistecon London SW1

April 8, 1978

Kal starts at The Economist

No Gulliver-he

Brezhnev understands only one language in Africa, page 11. Africans understand only one issue in southern Africa, page 13. Rhodesia's divided spoils, page 54. Russia's China distraction, page 58.

Eureka

China rediscovers science, page 57.

No, no neutron

President Carter's decision, page 26. His travels and return home, page 25.

Peaceniks

Now they are the fighters, page

Mr Healey's budget

Six pages of computer forecasts to 1983, a look back to 1974, and guesses for next week, pages 77-84. The Liberals' bid, page 17.

PR rides again

For Scotland, briefly, page 17. The poll in Garscadden, page 18.

Brittany's lessons

From the Amoco Cadiz, page 86.

France toujours

New French government, page 43. Old steel problem, page 88. Unusual car mileage, page 99.

Elections over-rigged

Marcos may, page 67. Desai couldn't, page 68. Bhutto is everybody's object lesson, page 67. But God spoke to Ghana's Acheampong, page 53.

Imports, please

India relaxes red tape, page 88.

Contents   Volume 267 Number 7023

11 No linkage in Lilliput
13 Southern African agenda
14 Education: Stop talking, please
15 Simple science

Britain
17 Labour's budget won't be Liberal enough; *Scotland; Garscadden by-election; Railwaymen; The monarchy; Hay-on-Wye; The arts*

The World
25 **American Survey:** Travelling is fun, but the real problems are at home; *Neutron bomb; Farming; South Carolina; Railways; Harvard; Atlanta; Hospitals*
43 **Europe:** France's new government; *Italy; Portugal; West Germany; Spain; Poland.* **European Community:** Reflation or hot air in Copenhagen?; *Currencies; Farms; Nuclear policy; Summertime; Eurocrats*
53 **International:** Ghana: April fooled; *Rhodesia; Cyprus and the Middle East; Israel; China; Russia and China; Philippines; Pakistan; India; Chile*

Business
71 **This week**
73 The new City watchdog
74 No consensus, so the yen rises
77 **Pre-budget:** Forward into the past?; *Forecasting Britain; The economic consequences of Mr Healey; Budget bets*
86 **International:** Now Brittany is hit by the black tide of recriminations; *India; French steel; German strike; Shipbuilding; American Motors; Pharmaceuticals*
100 **Schools Brief:** Social policies in Europe
103 **Britain:** Nationalised industries: telling them how it's going to be; *Stage four; Capital investment; Waste disposal; Leyland's soggy money; North Sea*
109 **Finance:** Four clearers in search of a tax break; *Hongkong and Shanghai/Marine Midland; State pensions; BOC International/Airco; Guest Keen and Nettlefolds*

Books
115 The National Theatre; *Oxford University Press; Henry Irving; Charles Dickens; Geoffrey Chaucer; Heinrich and Thomas Mann; The Lancashire cotton famine; Vichy France; International money*

Letters   4

In the Beginning

I arrived in the lobby of the London offices of The Economist in late March of 1978 for what I thought was my last shot at a career as a cartoonist.

I had landed in England the June before as a recent college graduate, leading a bicycle tour of American teenagers. After months of pedaling in the British Isles, I (all 5'9" of me) managed to secure an unlikely position as player and coach for the Brighton Basketball club.

While the team was winning on the court, it was losing in the bank. The team's financial difficulties forced me onto the streets, literally. I put my experience as college cartoonist for the Harvard Crimson to good use and drew caricatures of tourists on Brighton Pier and in London's Trafalgar Square for a whopping £2.00 ($3.00) a go.

But now the basketball season was drawing to a close. I had spent months visiting magazines and newspapers in London actively searching for cartooning opportunities with no luck. The Economist was my last stop before I'd have to give up and return stateside.

While in the lobby, I eyeballed the magazine. It was evident this was not going to be a good fit. In my portfolio were comic strips, animation and gag drawings. The Economist was staid, grey and visually turgid. The only art worth presenting was a series of published caricatures of obscure college professors I had penned the year before.

To my surprise those drawings piqued the interest of the Art director, Pip Piper. He asked to hold onto the caricatures so that he could share them with members of the editorial staff. A few days later I received a call from Pip asking if I would come back to the London offices to have a one day cartooning "trial."

It was to be on Wednesday, April 5 11:00 AM.

The night before, our team's two-hour basketball practice ended as scheduled at 10:00 PM. The lads and I then dashed to the pub before "time, gentlemen, please" was called by the landlord at 10:30 PM.

Over a pint or two, I asked my teammates to explain, in the allotted time, the basics of British politics to prepare me for my visit to The Economist in the morning.

Exasperated, the team recommended instead that I return to my flat that night and switch on BBC's "Newsnight," a topical current events program. As instructed, I sat in front of the telly, pad and pencil in hand as Newsnight featured an interview with the then-Chancellor of the Exchequer Denis Healey.

I listened and sketched. Fortunately, Mr Healey proved to be an excellent caricature subject whose generous eyebrows were a particular gift. I completed a satisfactory drawing of my first and only British politician before retiring for the evening.

The next morning I sat nervously in the 11th floor offices of The Economist awaiting my instructions. I had exhausted all prior hope of landing a cartooning job in the UK. I knew this was my one chance, one last chance to make it.

Then the word came of my assignment. Would I please draw a caricature of the Chancellor of the Exchequer, Denis Healey.

That's how it started.

That small drawing launched a long and happy marriage of cartoons and words on the pages of The Economist. Since that April day, I have published something near 4,000 drawings in the magazine.

I spent the next 10 years working in England contributing weekly to The Economist. I would come to the same St. James' Street building every Wednesday drawing caricatures of world leaders in pen and ink (see page 16).

In a few years' time I would be invited to create full colour renderings that would grace the cover of the magazine (see page 84). Twenty years later, now working in the US, I was honored to become The Economist's first editorial cartoonist, contributing a weekly satirical commentary on world news (page 126).

Today I operate out of a studio in my home in suburban Baltimore, Maryland. I arrived here in 1988 at the invitation of The Baltimore Sun, which had hired me to be their daily cartoonist. I accepted the job under the one condition: that I would continue to do my weekly cartoons for The Economist. This was no small feat.

In 1988 there was this new thing, you may have heard of it, called The Internet. Though no other artist had tried, The Economist's art director at the time, Aurobind Patel was eager to embrace this new technology to deliver my artwork from across the globe.

Our early experiments were not promising.

I would be required to drive an hour to Washington, DC to scan my cartoon. The work would then be sent to New Jersey where it would be outputted, scanned again then delivered to an address in London where The Economist would send a courier to collect. The results looked like mud.

Then we got a computer. A step in the right direction as I now could scan the cartoon myself. However to send a small black and white cartoon (about the size of a typically email today) from my home to London could take up to 3 hours... on international phone lines. An expensive endeavor.

Over the next 25 years, things have become dramatically faster and cheaper. Now, wherever I am in the world I will send my cartoons to The Economist every Wednesday. All I need is a laptop, portable scanner and an Internet connection.

It has been an enormous privilege to contribute to The Economist for all these years. I have worked with an impressive and distinguished group of colleagues. There are so many to thank for their contributions to my long and colorful career. *But none more than Denis Healey.*

Kal's first cartoon at The Economist.
08 April, 1978

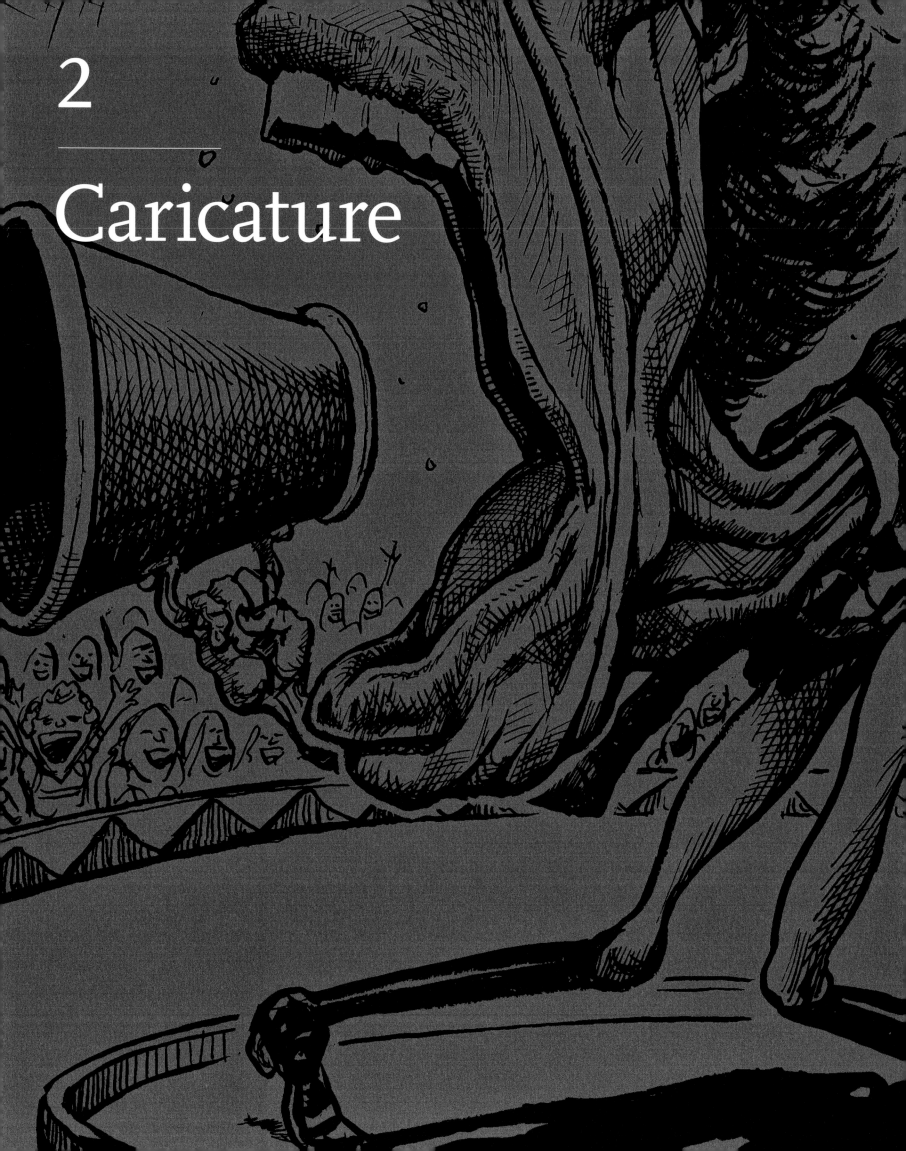

2

Caricature

Face Time

"A good caricature, like every work of art, is more true to life than reality itself."
Annibale Carracci (1560–1609)

Prior to joining The Economist, I peddled my wares as a street caricaturist drawing tourists in London's Trafalgar Square and Brighton's Palace Pier. There is no school for learning caricature, so this turned out to be an invaluable experience, as I could practice, learn and fine-tune the art of distortion with paying victims.

When I joined The Economist as their caricaturist in 1978, I discovered something new about the craft. I was no longer capturing the likeness of holiday-makers but instead was tackling the faces of policy-makers. My pen was now a potent weapon.

I quickly learned that diminishing a powerful politician through a withering caricature was one of the most powerful tools available to a cartoonist. Over time I have honed my caricature skills and pointed my poison pen at the faces of scores of world leaders. After 35 years, it may be fair to say, I have developed a weapon of mass distortion.

Mikhail Gorbachev
and Ronald Reagan
25 April, 1987

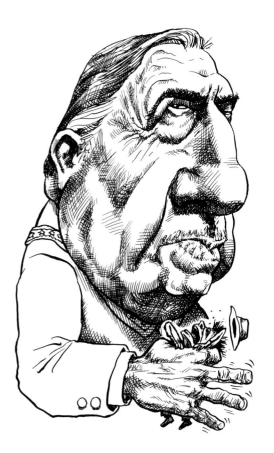

Augusto Pinochet, leader of the
military junta in Chile
22 June, 1985

Grand Ayatollah Ruhollah Khomeini,
Iran's Supreme Leader
15 January, 1983

Pope John Paul II
17 March, 1984

Gen. Norman Schwartzkopf, top
commander in the Persian Gulf War
1993

Vladimir Putin, president of Russia
20 October, 2007

Rock Musician Mick Jagger
20 January, 2001

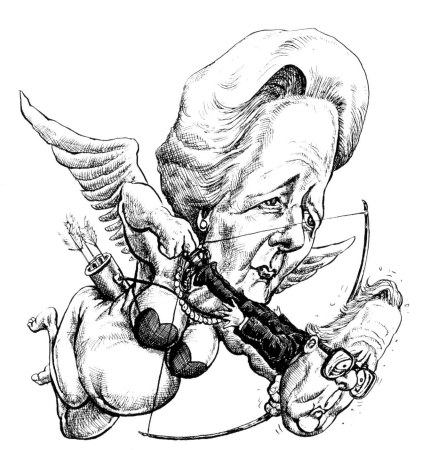

A menagerie of British prime ministers.

Margaret Thatcher, who served from 1979 to 1990, dispatching Foreign Secretary Sir Geoffrey Howe
12 July, 1986

Margaret Thatcher, with Neil Kinnock, long-time opposition leader
04 October, 1986

Tony Blair (1997-2007)
02 October, 2004

Gordon Brown (2007-2010)
28 February, 2009

John Major (1990-1997)
31 July, 1993

A herd of heads of state.

Indira Gandhi, India. Copies of
The Economist with this caricature
were confiscated in India.
25 August, 1984

Pervez Musharraf, Pakistan
10 November, 2007

KEVIN KALLAUGHER   DAGGERS DRAWN

Kim Jong Il, North Korea
07 December, 2002

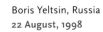

Boris Yeltsin, Russia
22 August, 1998

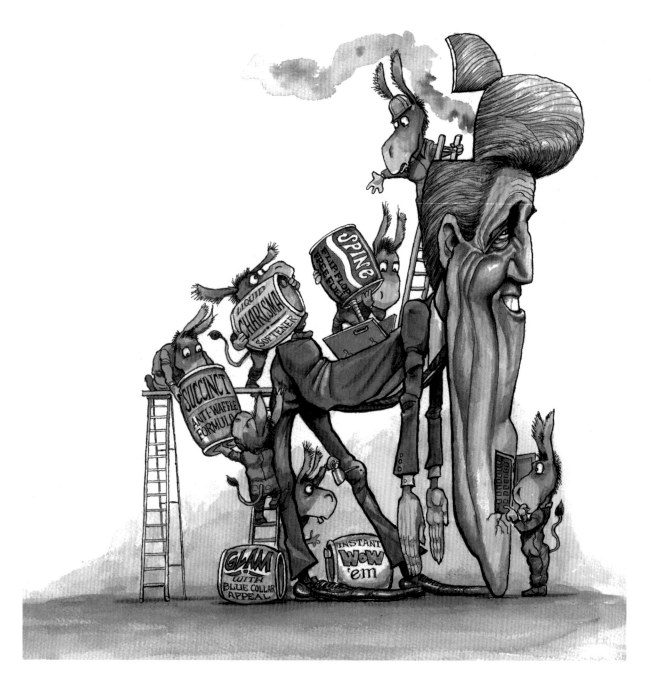

Presidential candidate John Kerry
24 July, 2004

Presidential candidate
Newt Gingrich
19 November, 2011

California Governor
Arnold Schwarzenegger and
George W. Bush
25 March, 2005

Republican presidential
nominee Mitt Romney and his
running mate, Paul Ryan
18 August, 2012

Secretary of State Hillary Clinton
13 January, 2007

Donald Trump, the real estate
mogul, briefly considered a run
for president.
23 April, 2011

A quartet of American presidents.

Jimmy Carter (1977-1981)
undated

Bill Clinton (1993-2001)
15 November, 1997

George W. Bush (2001-2009)
05 January, 2008

Barack Obama (since 2009)
17 October, 2009

3

United States

Star-Spangled Banter

"If you put the federal government in charge of the Sahara Desert, in five years there'd be a shortage of sand."
Milton Friedman

Over the past 35 years, hardy conservatives have reshaped the American political debate. "Government is not the solution to our problem," Ronald Reagan proclaimed at his first inauguration. "Government is the problem." Two Bushes followed, interrupted by Bill Clinton, who prevailed by leading the Democrats toward the center. And while Barack Obama won two terms, conservative opposition, led by clamorous Tea Party activists, created a counter-weight that kept government at the edge of crisis for extended periods.

A third party candidate, John Anderson, tangled with President Jimmy Carter, helping Ronald Reagan to sail to victory by a record margin for a non-incumbent.
10 April, 1980

Reagan led support for the Contras, an anti-communist guerilla group in Nicaragua.
15 March, 1986

Covert support for the Contras and a secret arms deal with Iran oozed together, creating a scandal that tarnished the once-untouchable Reagan. He now became a juicy target for Congressional opponents.
21 November, 1987

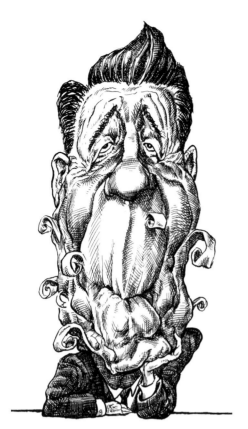

Reagan's legendarily impermeable "Teflon" coating began to sag in his second term.
05 May, 1985

Walter Mondale lacked staying power in his 1984 contest with Reagan.
1984

In 1988, Michael Dukakis and George H.W. Bush provided an uninspiring choice to succeed 8 years of Reagan.
10 September, 1988

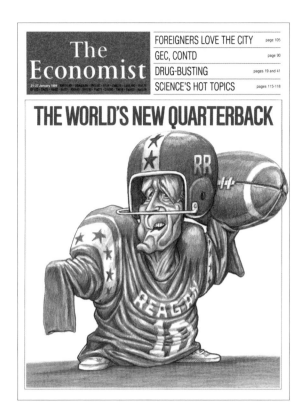

Michael Dukakis emerged as the Democratic nominee in 1988.
16 July, 1988

Bush prevailed by a substantial margin in the election, but it wasn't easy to match the stature of his predecessor.
21 January, 1988

Bush had a gentle, even posh, image, but turned aggressive when Iraq occupied Kuwait.
1990

06 June, 1992

Bill Clinton fought hard against the incumbent, George H.W. Bush, in 1992, while a third candidate, H. Ross Perot, entered and reshaped the fight. Clinton won, and went on to fight another day. His unsuccessful attempt to overhaul the national healthcare system left him badly bruised, and his party lost control of the House of Representatives in 1994 for the first time in 40 years.

20 August, 1994

Bill Clinton's critics on the left and right regarded him as a spineless waffler. But he was steadfast in his denials of wrongdoing during the controversy over his ill-advised relationship with intern Monica Lewinsky. While he tried to shape his legacy, Special Prosecutor Ken Starr had other plans.

Undated

18 January, 1997

KEVIN KALLAUGHER   DAGGERS DRAWN

In a spirited battle for the presidency, Al Gore and George W. Bush came close to a tie.

30 September, 2000

04 November, 2000

Third-party candidate Ralph Nader impeded Al Gore's path to the White House. After the ballots were cast, Gore and George W. Bush dueled for more than a month over the Florida recount, before a 5-to-4 Supreme Court decision made Bush the winner.

03 June, 2000

The terrorist attacks of 11 September, 2001, prompted mourning, followed quickly by a focus on security. George Bush, and later Barack Obama, controversially employed the US base at Guantanamo Bay as a detention center for alleged terrorist suspects.

15 September, 2001

Strategist Karl Rove helped call the tune for George W. Bush, but his dream of creating a permanent Republican majority hit a sour note.

16 July, 2005

18 August, 2007

George W. Bush was accused of performing for DC lobbyists.
07 December, 2002

Vice President Richard Cheney aggressively took aim at his administrations critics and accidently shot a friend while hunting quail.
18 February, 2006

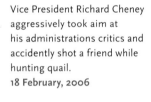

As in most American elections, the 2004 campaign hinged on the small number of states with a history of swinging between Democrats and Republicans.
07 August, 2004

After the legal disputes following the Bush-Gore election, all parties were geared up for a repeat in 2004. But the results were clearer, allowing Bush to claim victory on election night.
30 October, 2004

Bush's re-election revealed a more
marked shift toward conservatism.
06 November, 2004

George W. Bush tried to construct a "Star Wars" anti-missile system, with little success.
21 May, 2005

Harsh interrogation techniques, used to fight terrorism, were the subject of heated debates.
13 October, 2007

With Bush's popularity drained at the end of his term, Republican candidates in 2008 chose to keep their distance.
16 June, 2007

Immigration – legal and otherwise –
continued to impact US society.
A million legal permanent residents a
year helped shape the culture and
the political debate. Estimates of the
number of undocumented immigrants
ranged from 7 million to 20 million;
how to deal with them remained a
contentious issue.

14 January, 2006

24 August, 2002

26 February, 2011

Some dichotomies within American politics resurface periodically. Whether the issue is religion, privacy or secrecy, the particulars may change, but the underlying divisions remain.

14 May, 2011

15 November, 2003

28 May, 2005

03 March, 2012

Barack Obama outran a tenacious Hillary Clinton in the Democratic primary in 2008, but found the presidency slow going.

07 June, 2008

02 May, 2009

13 June, 2009

Vice President Joe Biden's mouth and brain were not in constant communication.
30 August, 2008

The neophyte Obama needed to grow into the job. As Commander-in-Chief, he tried to articulate a new doctrine on limited use of American power abroad.

26 June, 2010

02 April, 2011

At home, he encountered impatience with his economic policies and resistance on climate issues.

18 July, 2009

20 February, 2010

Dogs and cats. Troy and Sparta. And, since Thomas Nast's cartoons in the mid-19th Century, the Democratic donkey and the Republican elephant have been eternal antagonists.

24 March , 2001

16 April, 2011

Tea Party support in mid-term elections in 2010 brought aggressive Republicans to a majority in the House of Representatives, tipping the balance of power in Washington.
06 November, 2010

The division of power led to stalemates over budget, taxes and debt limits. Although both parties predicted dire consequences, neither was eager to compromise.
24 July, 2010

After passing sweeping health care reform in the House of Representatives, Speaker Nancy Pelosi looked to Democratic Senate Leader Harry Reid to bring the legislation home through the filibuster-prone upper house.
14 November, 2009

The small conservative Tea Party wing of the Republican Party exercised powerful influence, helping the GOP to regain control of the House of Representatives in 2010. Their uncompromising style caused consternation in and out of the party.

07 March, 2009

23 July, 2011

KEVIN KALLAUGHER   DAGGERS DRAWN

18 September, 2010

American style electioneering has become an unfortunate role model for other democracies. Over time, campaigns have become more expensive, vitriolic and amplified.

18 September, 2004

27 October, 2012

KEVIN KALLAUGHER *DAGGERS DRAWN*

The shooting of 20 Connecticut schoolchildren and six school staff members in December, 2012, reignited a debate on the role of firearms in American culture.

22 December, 2012

19 January, 2013

The 2012 campaign was one for the record books. It was the longest, most expensive and for the Republicans, possibly the most disappointing.

20 October, 2011

31 October, 2012

10 November, 2012

4

Europe

Coalition of the Somewhat Willing

"A day will come when we shall see... the United States of America and the United States of Europe face to face, reaching out for each other across the seas."
Victor Hugo

Many, including George Washington, had predicted it. European unity has come about. Up to a point. But the details and pace of unification, and questions over who would participate and to what degree, were and are still argued vociferously. In recent years, the Greek debt crisis, which threatened to diffuse itself to Spain, Portugal and Italy, provided the background for more hand-wringing over how – and even whether – European unity is viable.

Margaret Thatcher's Britain wouldn't stand for full European integration.
10 December, 1983

The Economic and Monetary Union, which created the Euro currency, was approved, some thought too soon, in 1998.

11 October, 1997

The Economist

OCTOBER 29TH–NOVEMBER 4TH 2011   Economist.com

Battle of the oil giants

Flat-tax plans for America

The West's decline in the Arab world

Student loans: the next bust?

Mind-reading becomes a reality

Europe's rescue plan

Rapid expansion, debt and mismanagement created an economic crisis in the EU. Recovery plans were put forward; some had more holes than others.

29 October, 2011

The US and Britain have long shared
a special relationship... that has had
its ups and downs.
07 March, 2009

No party won a majority in Britain's contentious 2010 election. The governing coalition, led by Conservative David Cameron, was immediately put to the test.
08 May, 2010

When Europe's fortunes appeared to be sinking, David Cameron proposed a UK referendum on withdrawal from the EU.
26 January, 2013

Speaking of unification, Kohl negotiated the bringing together of East and West Germany.
Undated

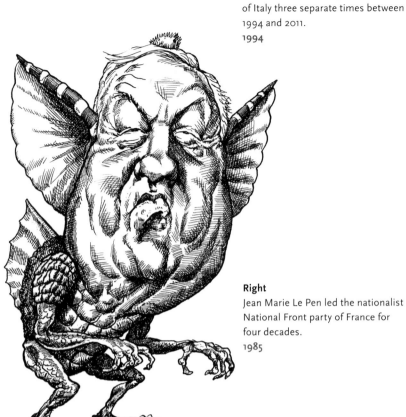

Left
Silvio Berlusconi was prime minister of Italy three separate times between 1994 and 2011.
1994

Right
Jean Marie Le Pen led the nationalist National Front party of France for four decades.
1985

European leaders met frequently, and frequently claimed they had the debt crisis under control.
27 November, 2010

Andreas Papandreou was a leading figure in opposition to Greece's military junta. After the country democratized, he became prime minister in 1981.

08 June, 1985

In recent years, it became clear the Greek government had fudged its books. The EU needed to bail it out, but arriving at a final deal was complex process. The Greek economy subsequently sputtered and citizens rebelled.

06 February, 2010

Germany's Angela Merkel took a stricter view of austerity than France's incoming leader, Francois Hollande.
12 May, 2012

Greece threatened to pull out of the EU over the austerity measures that came as conditions for its economic bailout.
18 August, 2012

Turkey's efforts to win membership in the EU were rebuffed several times; in 2005, it was Austria's objection that blocked it.
08 October, 2005

Needing energy, Europe was vulnerable to being squeezed by oil- and gas-producing states.
14 October, 2006

Mikhail Gorbachev was the last leader of the once dominant communist Soviet Union. When he came to power in 1988, he purged the party of the remnants of the Brezhnev era, shifted the Soviet Union into forward motion, and engaged with a wary Ronald Reagan.

27 July, 1987

31 January 1987

05 July, 1986

As president and as prime minister, Vladimir Putin has been the dominant figure in Russia and on the world stage since 1999.

18 September, 2004

02 November, 2002

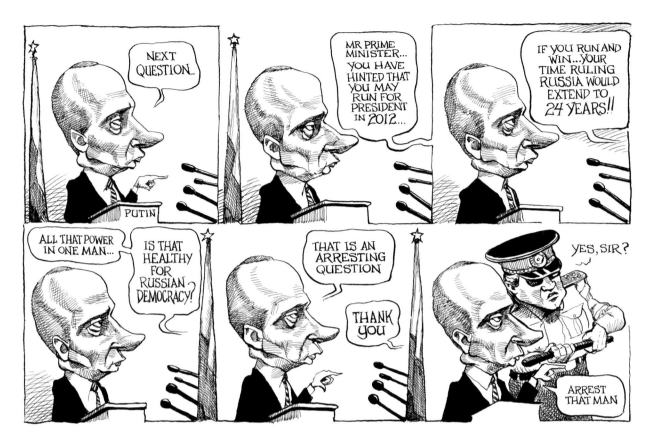

5

Economist Covers

The Front Page

The creation of The Economist's weekly cover is an amazing dance. It involves a handful of talented people working closely together on a tight deadline with complicated subjects for a very discerning audience.

I have had the pleasure to create more than 140 covers for The Economist over my career. It is a fast-paced, adrenaline-driven, thoroughly satisfying artistic experience... not without its minor mishaps.

My adventure usually starts with a notice when I rise in Baltimore on Monday morning instructing me to call London HQ. Hours earlier, the weekly meeting of the magazine's journalistic staff had convened in the office of the Editor to discuss the upcoming edition. A shortlist of possible cover subjects emerges, which is later reviewed by senior editors and graphic designers.

On any given week, there can be up to four different Economist covers being printed around the world. The Economist prints separate editions each week in the US, UK, Europe and Asia but also has the capability to make special editions for Latin America, Middle East and India. A typical week will have one cover going worldwide, but it is not unusual to have up to three separate covers being developed.

For example, The US edition may feature American budget talks, while the Europe edition spotlights Italian elections, and the Asia edition, Japanese economic reforms.

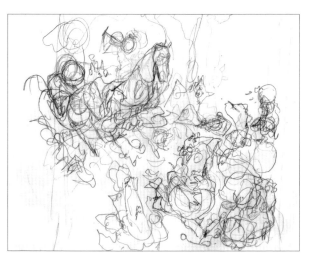

The cover artwork evolves from hieroglyphic scribbles to finished product in about 48 hours.

During my phone call with home base, I am offered an outline of the lead editorial (leader) that will determine what art will grace the cover. The illustration must work hand in hand with the leader, and, occasionally, a cartoon idea has been recommended for me to sketch. More often, I am asked to conjure some rough ideas on how to portray the week's leader in pictures.

I have worked closely for many years with the talented Graphics Editor, Penny Garrett, and Cover Designer Graeme James. I like first to bounce ideas off them, emailing sketches back and forth throughout Monday. By first thing Tuesday, the Editor gets involved in the process and a final concept and design are chosen. I now have 24 hours to paint and complete the artwork.

In my early years with the magazine I would often work at my home studio in the British seaside resort town of Brighton. Usually I would draw straight through the night, to maximize the hours available, then take a train to London to deliver the artwork on Wednesday. But one week, I remember facing an unusual challenge.

It was 1986. The reformer Mikhail Gorbachev had risen to lead the Soviet Union. He was the fresh new face of the Communist party. His open demeanor seemed shocking in comparison to the dour sourpusses we had become accustomed to over the decades.

I was entrusted to capture this modern new leader's image on the cover of The Economist. At the time, I was a fan of a new American TV show (viewed internationally) called Miami Vice. Excitingly, I had convinced my friends at The Economist to allow me to portray Gorbachev as a cool, hip kind of guy you might see on the show.

There was one problem with my scheme. It was Tuesday afternoon, and I had no picture reference for Miami Vice. Remember, this was before the internet enabled artists like me to cull thousands of images from the web. Back then, to help us with our artwork, we needed to build personal picture libraries made up of tear-sheets from newspapers and magazines as well as shelves full of reference books. Miami Vice was nowhere to be found in my library.

So I had no choice but to go shopping. My wife and I visited the shops in Brighton in search of a Miami Vice wardrobe. We quickly nabbed some duds, headed home then snapped a Polaroid photo of me modeling the new gear (see picture above). I worked through the night to complete the assignment using the photo as reference. The end result remains one of my favorite, and most expensive, covers (see picture at right).

The clothes were modeled upon the artists new possessions above. Sadly, the car was not.
26 July, 1986

Mikhail Gorbachev also played a major role in a cover near-calamity.

This was four years later and things had changed dramatically for Mikhail and me. I was now living in Baltimore, USA, and Gorbachev was overseeing what we now know was the dissolution of the Soviet Union.

While working in Baltimore, my timetable for delivering covers to London had evolved. I would get the customary call from London on Monday to discuss the cover. I would then need to complete the artwork by midday on Tuesday, when a courier would arrive at my house, collect the artwork and fly overnight to London to hand-deliver the goods.

This arrangement had been working well... up to that point. I had completed a nice painting for that week's edition featuring Gorbachev as a shepherd with his sheep abandoning him. I called the London office Wednesday morning eagerly awaiting their reaction. What I encountered was panic. They had learned the courier company had screwed up, and the artwork had never left the Baltimore airport. We had two hours to create a cover.

I grabbed my original pencil sketches. I hastily applied ink, and found a photocopier. I cut up the art into 6 pieces, enlarged each section on the photocopier to fill an A4 sheet, then faxed each sheet to London. (We were still in the pre-internet age.) There, the pieces were reassembled, photographed and quickly hand-coloured with an airbrush (see picture at right).

The deadline had been barely met, but London was not happy with either the courier company or the delivery system. So a new plan was devised: Each week when commissioned to do a cover for The Economist, I was to find a friend who would fly to London with my artwork in hand. The Economist would cover the round-trip airfare. As you can imagine, I suddenly had a lot of new friends.

A list was created with all the willing messengers. The list was long. Yet when it came time to call upon the volunteers, it was surprisingly hard to find someone on the list to make a transatlantic trip on 24 hours notice. We stumbled along with this quasi-courier service for a year or two. Thankfully, the magic of computers eventually allowed the digital transmission of cover artwork.

Today, I have become accustomed to transmitting my cover art from just about anywhere. I have delivered covers from the kitchen table of a dude ranch in Wyoming and a hotel room in Rome.

Over the years, The Economist has become well known for its intelligent and entertaining covers. Although the delivery method has changed dramatically, the challenge to provide an engaging front cover remains the same. It is a great honour when that challenge is entrusted to me.

Though I have done it 140 times before, drawing a cover for The Economist gives me a special kind of pleasure. When I get that notice from HQ on Monday morning that a cover is in the works, I know the amazing dance is about to start.

A makeshift cover for a downshifting Soviet Union.
13 January, 1990

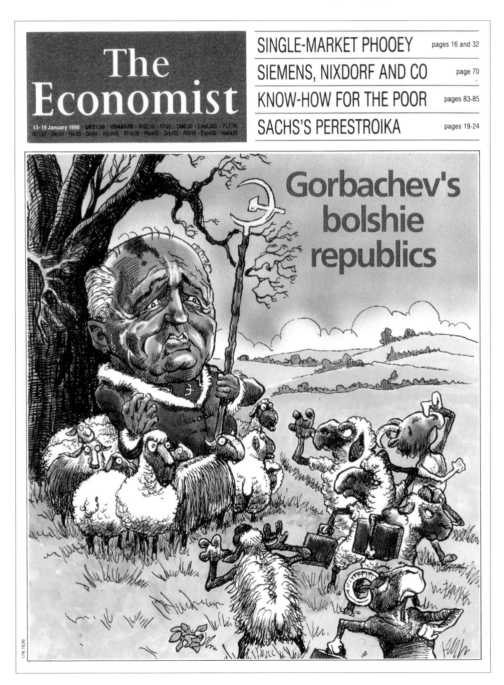

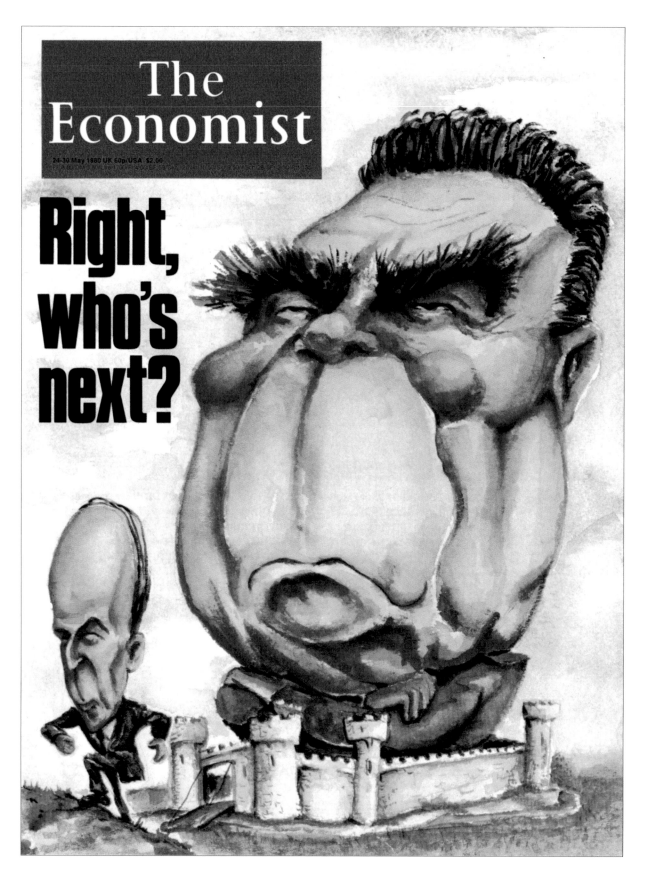

Leaders of the world's two superpowers, Leonid Brezhnev of the Soviet Union and US President Ronald Reagan went head-to-head.

This cartoon was Kal's first Economist cover.
24 May, 1980

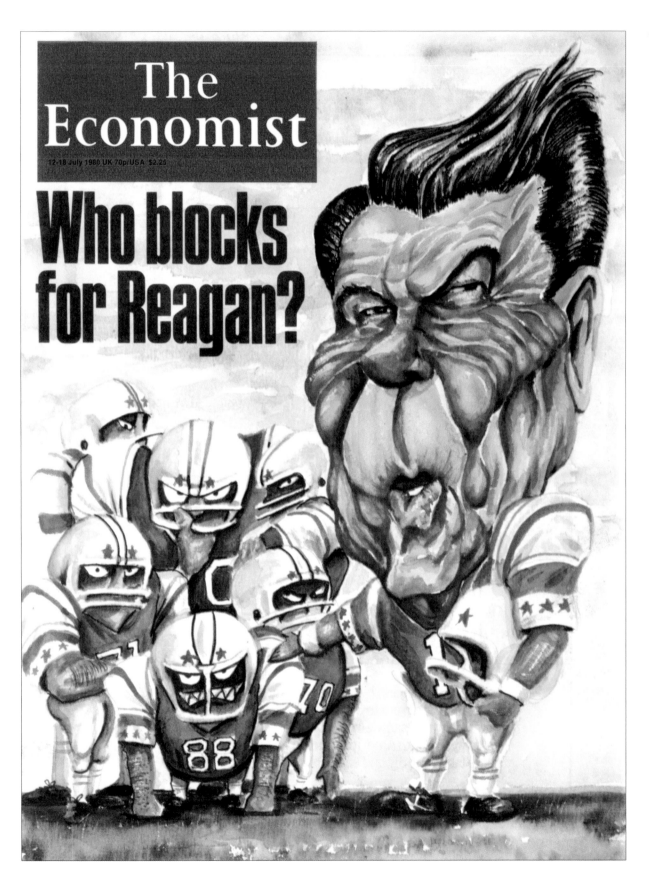

The indomitable Margaret Thatcher led the Conservatives to victory in three consecutive British elections and imposed a different vision on the country's economy and society.

04 November, 1989

17 March, 1990

So much to do

06 June, 1987

Four decades of the Cold War made relations between the East and the West testy.
07 November, 1987

New age communist leaders
Mikhail Gorbachev and
Deng Xiaoping changed things
by introducing economic
reforms, bypassing Marx and Mao.
01 June, 1991

The Economist

7-13 November 1987 · UK£1.30 · USA$3.00 · IR£1.90 · FF18 · DM6.00 · Lire5,000 · FL6.50
BF107 · Dkr22 · Nkr20 · Skr21 · ASch42 · SFr5.00 · Pts350 · Drs350 · FIM15 · Esc375 · Naira11

DOLLAR'S DIVE	page 14
LAWSON EXPECTS	page 15
JERUSALEM'S WAY	pages 23-26
OUR SLUMP BAROMETER	page 74

Putting
the rev in
revolution

WHEN CHIRAC CRACKED
GORBACHEV'S ROVING EYE
ALLIES AFTER IRAGUA: OUR POLL
JAPANESE TAX REFORMS

Lordy me

The Economist

BUSHAKIS WINS DEBATE
SHRINKING NASA
DEATH OF LEBANON
DOLLAR'S BERLIN WALL

There was only one problem

The Economist

BANKS IN TROUBLE
THE GOOD CHEMISTRY GUIDE
POLL TAX RETURNS
CLEANING UP
A survey of industry and the environment

Five weeks later...

The Economist

SPAIN'S EMS LESSONS
A HARDER ISRAEL
GREEN DIPLOMACY
ONLY COMMUNICATE
A survey of information technology

The warm war

The Economist

SELLING BOSNIA
CALIFORNIA ROARS BACK
PROGRESS ON ULSTER
HOW TO WIN IN CHINA

START

The Republicans' choice

The Economist

WHY WORK SO LONG?
WRONGS IN CUBA

Which Bill Clinton?

The Economist

Catching Karadzic
Sarkozy gets it right
Nudging the British to behave better
NASA at 50
How hedge funds are doing

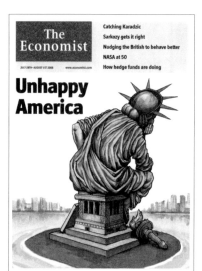

Unhappy America

The Economist

Beijing's nightmare: the Uighur revolt
The public-sector pension scam
The surge in Afghanistan
Eat less, live longer: it's true
Don't protect bad Belgian art

America's future
California v Texas

The Economist

Obama's first 100 days
Latin America's economic resilience
Pakistan attacks the Taliban
Wall Street's angry shareholders
The dancing parrot

The pandemic threat
How scared should you be?

Let the
dollar drop

Business in America
Its next problem:
Big Government

PLUS A 14-PAGE SPECIAL REPORT

The euro crisis:
time for Plan B

WHAT TO
DO ABOUT
GLOBAL
WARMING
pages 22 and 87-93

The making of a president

Surprise!
The power of the
emerging world

The oiloholics

Show me
the way
to go
home

Still
No.1

Time to get tough
Lessons from Obama's first year

The Economist

JANUARY 18TH - 24TH 1997

IRAN
A survey after page 54

COSTING
COMPUTERS
page 61

OUR THRILLER
SOLVED
page 83

Think big, Mr President

Bill Clinton was sworn in for a
second term in 1997, but any big
plans he had were largely derailed
by the Monica Lewinsky scandal
and by an aggressive Republican
Congressional majority.
18 January, 1997

KEVIN KALLAUGHER   DAGGERS DRAWN

A cover takes shape:
sketch, painting, final product.
15 January, 2011

George W. Bush, a novice in foreign affairs, was introduced to complex conflicts in Asia and the Middle East...

17 February, 2001

16 March, 2002

KEVIN KALLAUGHER   DAGGERS DRAWN

As his Iraq war dragged on, George Bush's stature and influence diminished.

29 May, 2004

KEVIN KALLAUGHER   DAGGERS DRAWN

24 February, 2007

11 November, 2006

Barack Obama faced mid-term anger, a sharp-elbowed re-election campaign, and controversy over the bailout of troubled banks and automakers.

30 October, 2010

14 April, 2012

KEVIN KALLAUGHER   DAGGERS DRAWN

The uncompromising Tea Party faction made life difficult for the Democrats – and often for the Republicans.
12 June, 2010

Conservatives struggled to find a candidate with an appealing mix of political positions and personality traits.
31 December, 2011

The Economist's year-end covers are often intricate, and Hieronymus Bosch is no longer available to paint them.
22 December, 2012

An Asian economic crisis produced a "mini-crash" on the stock market in 1997, wiping out a trillion dollars in market value in one October day.
01 November, 1997

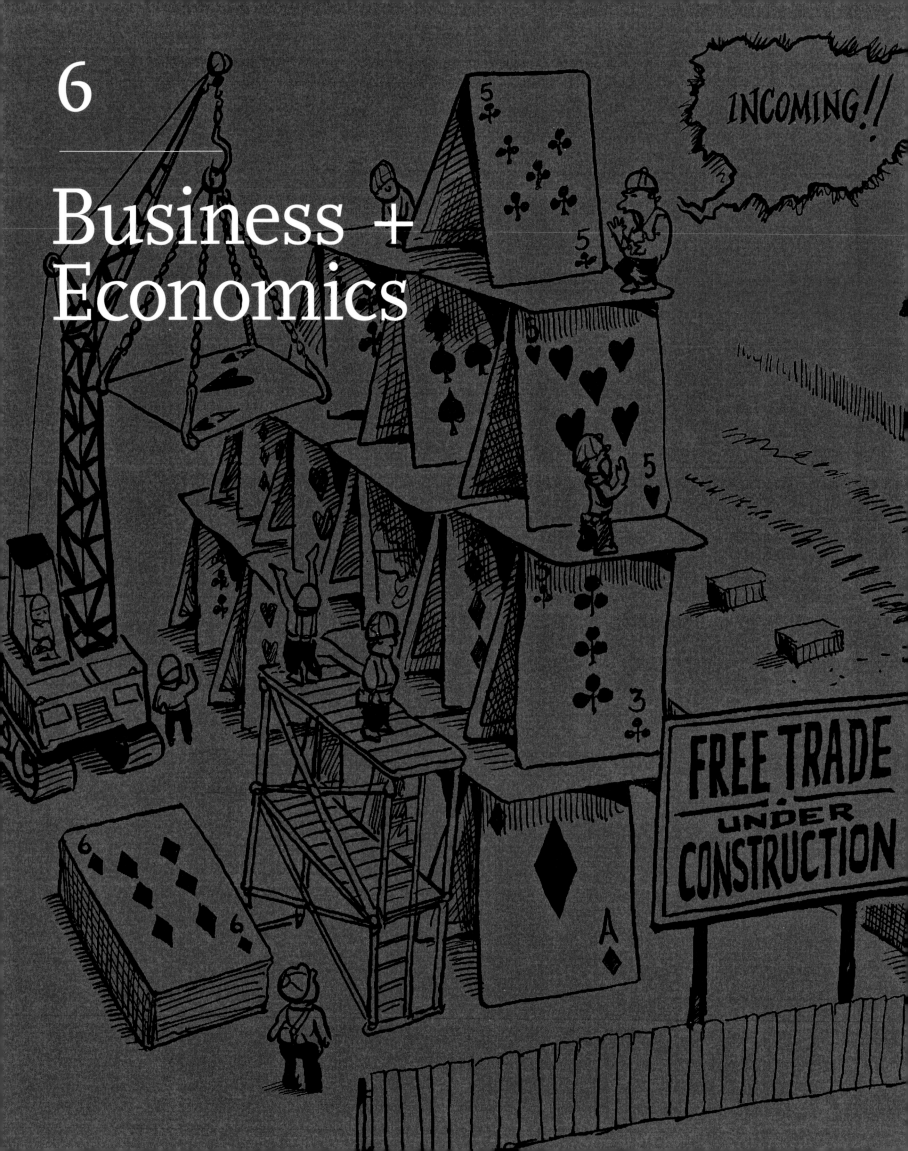

Upside Down

"The process by which banks create
money is so simple that the mind is repelled."
John Kenneth Galbraith

The fanciest new processes by which banks created
money – subprime mortgages, collateralized debt
obligations, mortgage-backed securities – sometimes
proved more complex than imagined by Galbraith – and
also more repellant. Bankers got bailed out but for the
rest of us, the 2008 crash pushed the world's economies
into the deepest recession since the Great Depression.

31 October, 1987

A deep recession in the US in 2008 reverberated around the world.

26 January, 2008

The recession proved stubborn. Counter-measures often seemed unavailing or created unintended consequences.

20 November, 2010

03 May, 2008

25 July, 2009

*The chairman of the Federal Reserve –
the head of the central bank for
the world's largest economy – often
seemed a larger-than-life figure.*

At times, Paul Volcker
appeared more powerful than
even Ronald Reagan.
11 February, 1984

Alan Greenspan guided a bumpy
economy to a soft landing.
1995

Aside from his reputation as a cryptic oracle, Greenspan was at first seen as rescuer of the economy.
21 April, 2001

YOU'LL INHERIT A HEALTHY GROWTH RATE... LOW UNEMPLOYMENT...

THE FED

AND A HOUSING BUBBLE

Bernanke

When Ben Bernanke replaced Greenspan, he inherited more than the job.
29 January, 2005

The Clinton-era budget surplus
shrank after tax cuts and war-fueled
spending increases.
13 October, 2007

The recovery beginning in 2009 saw accelerated economic growth, share prices and corporate profits, but jobs continued to lag.
31 October, 2009

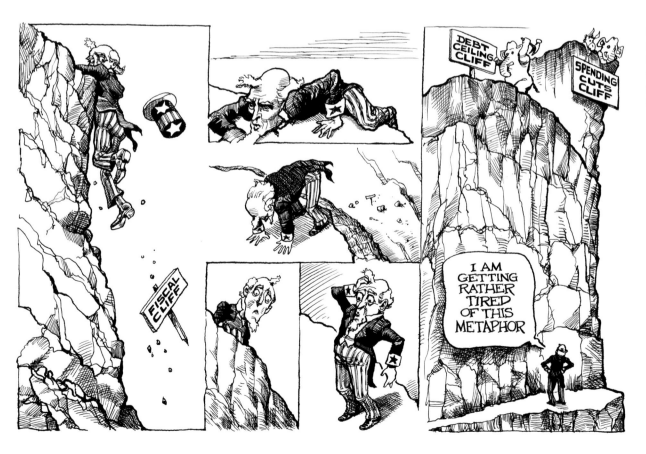

A combination of tax increases and spending cuts threatened to plunge the US economy back into recession at the end of 2012. An 11th-hour deal deferred the crisis by a few months.
05 January, 2013

Amid economic ups and downs, the conduct of those at the top – and the lavish rewards they pocketed – drew attention and criticism.

01 May, 2010

24 April, 2010

A press baron, Rupert Murdock, came out of Australia to collect media properties in the UK and around the world.
1984

His purchase of the respected Wall Street Journal raised fears of political interference in news coverage.
23 June, 2007

Hacking and snooping by his staff
led to investigations, including
embarrassing disclosures of close
(and sometimes paid) relations
with public officials.
23 July, 2011

Rising oil prices in 2004 threatened economic recovery.

29 May, 2004

03 April, 2004

KEVIN KALLAUGHER   DAGGERS DRAWN

The recession stimulated talk about capitalism's ills, although capitalism seemed to have the last word.

18 October, 2008

21 July, 2012

The world searched for a formula
for fair trade...
11 May, 2002

And searched.
02 August, 2008

And searched.
16 February, 2013

7

International

Tangled

"Love is like war: easy to begin but very hard to stop."
H.L. Mencken

The US and its allies entered wars in Iraq, Afghanistan, and then Iraq again. Determined to promote "nation-building," they found that some nations resist being built, or, at least, resist being built by others. Elsewhere, tyrants came and went, or came and didn't go; either way, tyranny often persisted. The Soviet Union fell; China rose. There was promise in South Africa and in the Arab Spring, but the promise wasn't easily fulfilled.

15 October, 2011

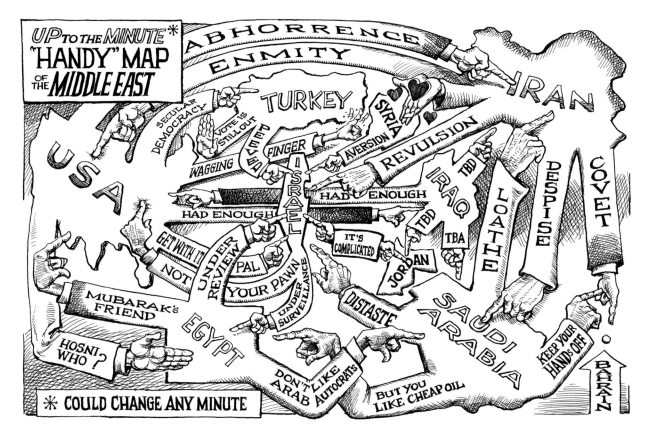

Iraq's Saddam Hussein threatened to invade neighbouring Kuwait, spooking global gas prices.
04 August, 1990

In the wake of the 9/11 terrorist attacks, the US began hunting for Osama Bin Laden, but quickly turned its attention to the outlaw Saddam Hussein.
01 Decmeber, 2001

Sketchy intelligence was used to justify the invasion of Iraq.

This drawing was named Cartoon of the Year in Great Britain in 2004.
15 July, 2004

Britain eagerly joined the US in the Iraq venture, but other countries were ambivalent.

06 April, 2004

06 September, 2003

 DAGGERS DRAWN

The US and allies staged a successful invasion, but were less equipped for "nation-building."

05 April, 2003

22 March, 2003

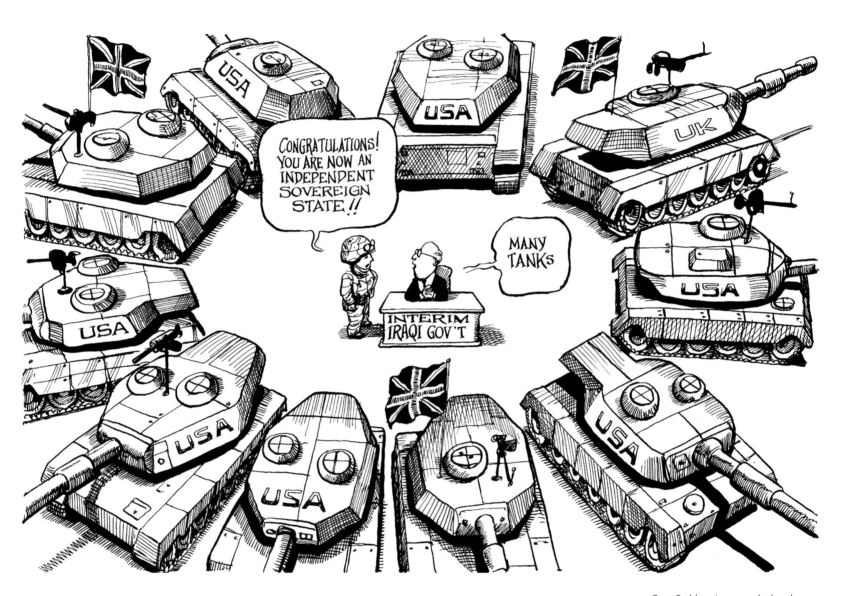

Post-Saddam Iraq was declared
sovereign, but depended on
us and uk forces to keep order.
03 July, 2004

After four years Iraq remained unstable. A new influx of troops helped stabilize the country, but encouraged enemies elsewhere.
15 September, 2007

With great fanfare and trepidation the US and its allies announced the withdrawal of their forces from Iraq.
07 August, 2010

A month after the 9/11 attacks, the US and its allies began a war in Afghanistan with high hopes.
27 October, 2001

The US had trouble persuading other countries to help finance the Afghan project.
19 April, 2003

President Hamid Karzai's government had little effective control outside of Kabul.
11 December, 2004

The coalition entered Afghanistan in earnest, but withdrawing proved to be tricky.

02 February, 2008

21 April, 2012

The former Governor of Texas found
foreign policy hard work.

04 June, 2005

Jimmy Carter mediated the Camp David agreement between Israel's Menachem Begin and Egypt's Anwar Sadat, at great political risk to all three.
05 July, 1980

After the assassination of Sadat in 1981, Hosni Mubarak dominated Egypt until he was ousted in the 2011 Arab Spring.
31 October, 1987

As Israel's minister of defense, Ariel Sharon replaced a tradition of intelligent soldiery with blunter methods in a 1982 invasion of Lebanon.
09 October, 1982

Yasser Arafat, head of the Palestine Liberation Organization, proved to be an adept political survivor but a lousy leader.
09 June, 2001

The US tried sporadically to broker peace in the Middle East, but Israel often steered its own course.

12 April, 2003

The only thing that is certain in the Middle East is constant uncertainty.

11 October, 2003

17 November, 2012

27 October, 2012

The quirky and troublesome Muammar Qaddafi ruled Libya after a 1969 coup.
04 April, 1987

Much of the world rejoiced when European nations aided Libyans in the overthrow of the dictator. Others were less keen.
26 February, 2011

Hafez Assad controlled Syria
for 30 years.
03 May, 1986

Hafez Assad's son, Bashar Assad,
continued attacking his own
people, ignoring Western threats.
31 May, 2012

Iran's Islamic Republic, with its nuclear ambitions, confounded the West.

14 February, 2004

31 July, 2004

With a variety of weapons and methods, terrorists stalked the world. The invasions of Iraq and Afghanistan tried and failed to blunt the threat.

15 August, 1998

15 August, 1998

29 September, 2007

29 July, 2006

Jean-Claude "Baby Doc" Duvalier inherited Haiti's dictatorship from his father.
18 February, 1984

Cuba's Fidel Castro tried to present a positive picture of his brand of outdated communism.
07 May, 1988

Hugo Chavez, Venezuela's strong man known for his idiosyncratic brand of socialism, died in 2013 after 14 years in power.
10 March, 2103

Luiz Inácio Lula da Silva won re-election as president of Brazil, despite challenges.
16 July, 2005

Mexican President Felipe Calderon found an uncertain ally in his bloody battle against drug cartels.
30 October, 2010

A series of international conferences, including ones in Copenhagen in 2009 and Doha in 2012, failed to produce agreement on strong action to limit climate change.

21 November, 2009

A study finding oil and gas near the North Pole touched off debates over who owned the mineral rights. The cartoon isn't as metaphorical as you might think; great powers sent submarines to survey the area and stake claims.
18 August, 2007

08 December, 2012

Kofi Annan served a decade as Secretary-General of the United Nations. He won a Nobel Peace Prize in 2001, but his efforts only occasionally met with success.

26 March, 2005

16 December 2006

Paul Wolfowitz, an architect of the Iraq War, was named president of the World Bank in 2006. He was pressured out of office in 2007.
21 April, 2007

The G-8, a group of the world's wealthiest and developed countries, hosted an annual summit in Berlusconi's Italy.
04 July, 2009

In the world of sports, there was a continuing cycle of doping accusations and denials.

14 August, 2004

28 July, 2007

KEVIN KALLAUGHER   DAGGERS DRAWN

After terrorist attacks, airport security became more rigid, forcing flyers to become more flexible.
09 January, 2010

The Roman Catholic Church was buffeted – from without and within – by sex abuse scandals.
03 April, 2010

The border between India and
Pakistan remains the world's most
dangerous. India's Indira Gandhi
and Pakistan's Zia ul Haq gingerly
tried to defuse tensions.
04 June, 1983

Rajiv Gandhi succeeded his mother
when she was assassinated; he was
felled by a suicide-bomber seven
years later.
12 March, 1988

Pakistan's Pervez Musharraf and India's Atal Bihari Vajpayee initiated talks to resolve the dispute over the contested border region of Kashmir.
14 July, 2001

The killing of Osama bin Laden in 2011 complicated US relations with Pakistan even further.
07 May, 2011

North Korea remained a cocooned and isolated troublemaker. Kim Jung Un replaced his father, Kim Jung Il, as North Korea's Supreme Leader in 2011. The change made no difference. The bellicose country continued to mistreat its citizens and cock its nose at the world.

26 October, 2002

25 September, 2010

14 April, 2012

Corazon Aquino led the "People Power Revolution" to overthrow the Marcos dictatorship. She was president of the Philippines from 1986 to 1992.
12 September, 1987

Lee Kuan Yew became prime minister when Singapore gained autonomy in 1959. During three decades in power, he built the tightly-controlled country into an economic powerhouse.
28 May, 1988

Junichiro Koizumi, prime minister
from 2001 to 2006, tried to get
Japan's once formidable economy
back into shape.
16 June, 2001

Guerilla leader Jonas Savimbi helped overthrow the colonial government of Angola in 1975, then fought a long civil war against the new government, led most of that time by Jose Eduardo dos Santos. Savimbi was killed in a battle with government troops in 2002.

02 December, 1999

01 July, 1989

THE CHEATAH

Robert Mugabe, a leader in overthrowing white-minority rule in Rhodesia, became president of the renamed Zimbabwe in 1980. He presided over political and ethnic tensions, periodically erupting into warfare. He was accused of vote-rigging, and destroying the economy with his land-redistribution policies.

23 March, 2002

17 March, 2007

AT LEAST THE COUNTRY IS NO LONGER MOVING BACKWARDS

P.W. Botha tried to preserve by force the white-minority regime of South Africa. His successor, F.W. de Klerk, freed Nelson Mandela and brought an end to the apartheid government. Mandela won the first multi-racial election.
21 June, 1986

I AM A MUCH BETTER FIT FOR THE JOB THAN YOU!

ZUMA

MBEKI

PROPERTY of NELSON MANDELA

The successor to the country's charismatic liberation leader, Nelson Mandela, was Thabo Mbeki who served two uninspired terms as president. Jacob Zuma was his deputy, then his political rival. Zuma won the presidency in 2009.
27 September, 2008

An ethnically-based decade-long civil war in the Darfur province of Sudan produced 300,000 deaths and 4 million displaced persons. The United Nations was accused of reacting slowly to the humanitarian crisis.
25 September, 2004

Democracy spread around the globe, but not always smoothly.

26 January, 2008

Mahmoud Ahmadinejad of Iran, Hamid Karzai of Afghanistan, Robert Mugabe of Zimbabwe

31 December, 2011

07 November, 2009

As "paramount leader" of China for a generation beginning 1978, Deng Xiaoping initiated economic reforms but resisted political change.
01 July, 1989

GOOD NEWS!!
CHINA IS ACQUIRING A TASTE FOR DEMOCRACY!!!

THE BAD NEWS IS.. I'M THE DEMOCRACY

TAIWAN

Tensions flared periodically between China and Taiwan, its democratic island neighbour.
19 March, 2005

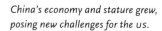
China's economy and stature grew, posing new challenges for the us.

14 November, 2009

17 April, 2010

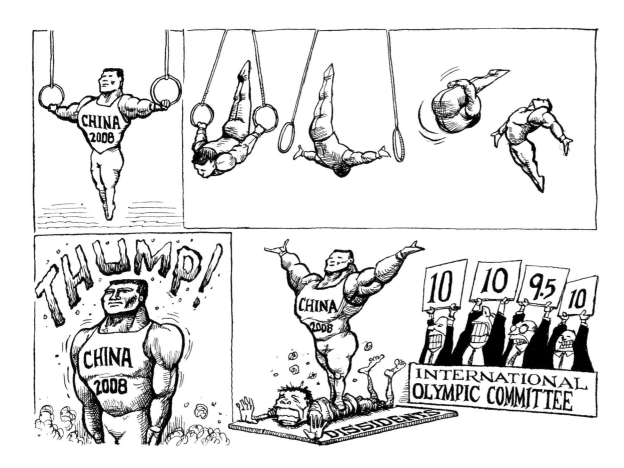

China was awarded the 2008 Olympic Games despite concerns over human rights abuses in the secretive society.

21 July, 2001

09 August, 2008

KEVIN KALLAUGHER   DAGGERS DRAWN

The Chinese government was angered when Liu Xiaobo, a human rights activist, won the 2010 Nobel Peace Prize.
16 October, 2010

Modern warfare moved into a dangerous new theatre.

09 May, 2009

23 February, 2013

Security-conscious governments attempted, with mixed success, to control information in the new internet age.

29 October, 2011

22 September, 2012

8

Kal's Projects with The Economist

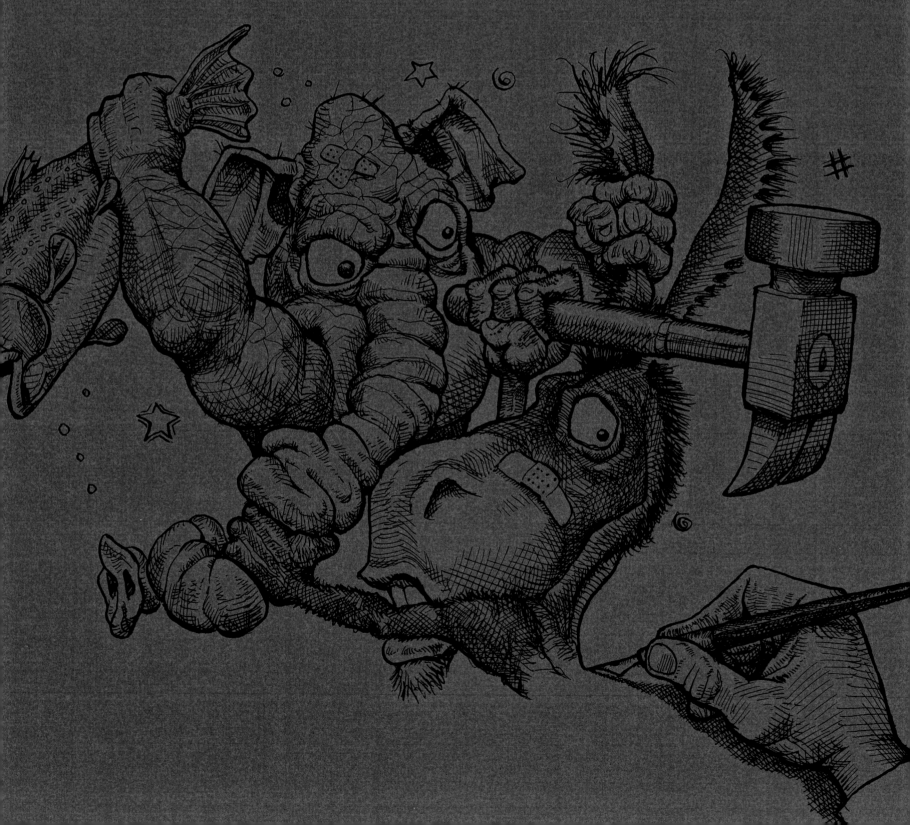

Out and About

When I first joined The Economist in 1978, the circulation was hovering around 300,000. Today it is six times that. As the magazine's star has risen around the globe, I have been a happy beneficiary. My cartoons have been showcased on a large stage to an international audience under a bright spotlight.

As the profile of The Economist has grown, I have often been called upon to make the most of my time on stage. This includes promoting the brand through special projects. When The Economist invites me to join a new project, I accept with delight. On behalf of the magazine, I have created calendars, animations and a board game, toured the US with The Second City improv comedy troupe and addressed audiences around the world.

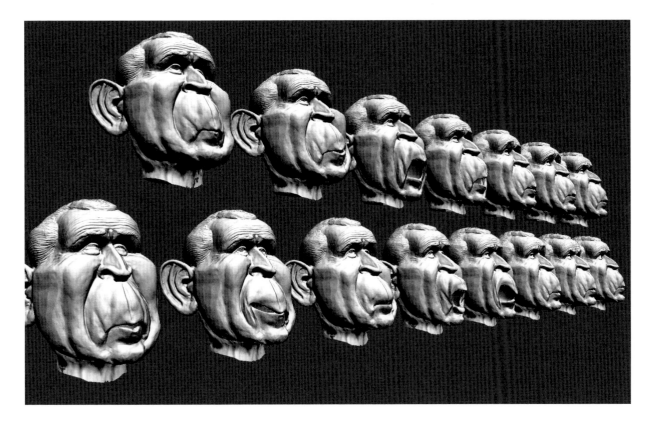

Kal's "Digital Dudya" being prepared for animation.
2006

Game Time

The annual end-of-year double edition of The Economist is a special treat for readers. It is packed full of special features and thought-provoking essays. In 2008, the editor of the special edition, Emma Duncan, asked me to pitch her an idea for that year's issue. We were in the throes a world economic meltdown at the time. I thought it might be good to use the graphic simplicity of a cartoon to try to explain how we got into this complicated mess.

Together, Emma and I settled on a solution. We conspired to create "Credit Crunch," a winner-take-all multiplayer board game that would be the center spread of the magazine.

Designing a game is no small task, as we discovered. In addition to contriving the intricate art of the board and currency (the Econo), the plot and rules of the game needed to be created and employed. We beta-tested and tweaked the game with friends and family. When the game was finally published, readers could go to The Economist website and download money, rules and financial risk cards.

The game was a hit with readers. We had requests for the game to be translated into other languages and coded into a computer game. Credit Crunch is still available online at *www.Economist.com/boardgame.*

Prior to printing, the board game went through many iterations, which involved adjusting artwork, evolving rules and changing the game's name.
December, 2008

The board game was designed for the special year-end edition of The Economist. On the left half of the board players earn money and power at an alarming rate and lose it at the same speed on the right half. Winners relish their hometown being named after them, losers languish in Chapter 11.

20 December, 2008

Kalendar

Among the fun projects I have participated in over the years, my series of Economist wall calendars was perhaps the most challenging. The first of three was made in 2009 for the 2010 calendar year. The original proposal was to create a simple wall calendar that would reproduce my previously published cartoons from the magazine above a standard monthly grid. However, when I heard about the project my mind exploded with ideas.

How about something a little more ambitious, I thought. Perhaps I could make a special calendar packed full of interesting facts and fun dates, elaborately illustrated and hand-lettered throughout! I enthusiastically created a sample monthly spread and luckily got the commission. The only problem now was that I had to complete this gargantuan task.

After six months of late nights and long days chained to the drawing board, the first calendar was complete. The effort paid off, as the product was well received including being named a finalist for Calendar of the Year by the Calendar Marketing Association. Two more calendars followed, with more, I hope, in the pipeline.

The wall calendar featured factual and whimsical dates and anniversaries. Readers were encouraged to match the dates below with the corresponding events above. Extra points for locating the artist who resides, like Waldo, in each spread. ˉ 2012

On stage

In addition to being a year of economic turmoil, 2008 was a presidential election year in the us. The Economist has a significant part of its circulation in the us, and that year, a nationwide marketing push was under way to expand it. To help promote the magazine a special stage show called "The Art of Satire" was created. The Economist teamed up with the famous improv comedy company The Second City for a six-city tour culminating with two shows on the weekend before the November election in Times Square, NYC.

I was asked to be the face of The Economist for the tour. It had been my privilege to represent the magazine at many public appearances over the years, addressing audiences in theaters, in conferences and on campuses. When I was invited to join this project, I knew something special would be required.

I had been experimenting with the use of live interactive animation in my role as an Artist-in-Residence at University of Maryland Baltimore County (UMBC). At UMBC, I had built a 3-D version of George W. Bush, dubbed the Digital Dubya, based on my drawings and a life-sized sculpture (see below). For The Economist's stage show I plotted to take Dubya a step further and utilize new motion capture technology to make him and other cartoon characters come alive for the audience.

The performers from Second City and I created a tantalizing set-up. We would have a live improv press conference between the audience and the digital president (on screen). A cast member would be on stage moderating the exercise, while I would be backstage in a motion capture suit miming the actions and doing a voice impersonation of Dubya. It worked. The performance with its topicality and spontaneity was one of the highlights of the program.

Buoyed with success, when the show came to the Yerba Buena Arts Center in San Francisco, we decided to take the project up a notch.

By now we had created 3-D digital models of Hillary Clinton, Barack Obama and John McCain. For this show I proposed a new context... a dance contest between Obama and McCain. The audience would choose the dance styles (Ballet, hip hop, disco etc.), a musician on stage would perform a quick succession of tunes, and I, outfitted in a motion capture suit backstage, would dance in character (see picture at right). It was a hit. After each digital candidate did his number on screen the audience enthusiastically cast its vote. Not surprisingly, Obama won this one-of-kind presidential contest.

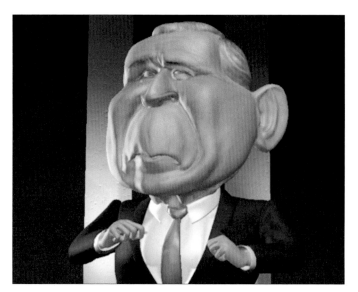

As an Artist-in-Residence at UMBC Kal designed a digital Dubya that came alive using motion capture technology.

As part of the nationwide tour with The Second City, Kal performed a stand-up cartoonist routine that included a drawing lesson for the audience.

At the San Francisco show, Kal teamed with PhaseSpace motion capture company to do a live dance contest between digital caricatures of Barack Obama and John McCain

Audience queues for two sold out "Art of Satire" shows in New York's Time Square.

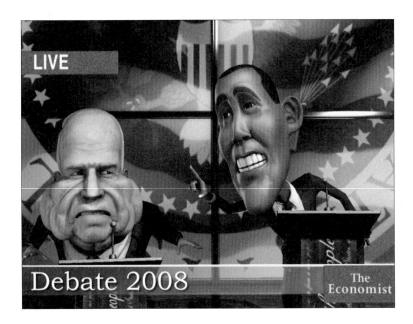

Kal worked with software studio Digital Steamworks to create a series of 3-D animated projects. Digital versions of contemporary politicians were built modeled on clay sculptures and sketches by Kal, then cast in animated shorts.

Presidential debate, New York City.
02 November, 2008

John McCain
2008

Hillary Clinton
2008

Very moving

When I graduated from Harvard in 1977, my senior thesis was a 13-minute animated cartoon based upon a comic strip that I had penned in the school newspaper. Since then, I have remained a huge fan of animation and the special power that it can deliver. It has been a life-long ambition for me to find a way to successfully merge the magic of animation with the topicality of political cartooning. Now, with the advance of computers and software, that dream is becoming a reality.

I have embarked on new animation projects with The Economist. First there was a 3-D animation that employed same digital characters from the stage show. We produced a four-minute film that featured a game show style debate titled "The 2008 Debate we would really like to see."

More recently, I have been exploring traditional (2-D) animated cartoons. This includes a series of two-minute films that set out to explain, using humour, some commonly used economic terms (debt, taxes, hyper-inflation etc.).

As print publications such as The Economist move increasingly to digital formats and platforms, the opportunities for animation will grow. With the swelling popularity of tablets, smartphones and other digital devices, I believe satirical animated shorts will one day be as prevalent as political cartoons have been print. I am looking forward to exploring new exciting animation projects with The Economist as we move together into the digital age.

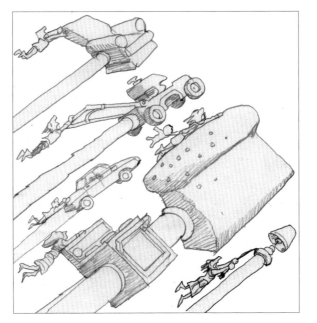

Kal worked with Baltimore based Bully Entertainment to create a series of animated films based on terms gleaned from The Economist's book "Essential Economics: An A to Z Guide."

Top
Economic bubbles, including tulip mania in 17th century Holland, are featured in one short.
2013

Center and Bottom
Skyrocketing hyperinflation may be bad for countries but it is good for animation.
2013

About the Cartoonist

Kevin Kallaugher

Kevin Kallaugher (Kal) is the international award-winning editorial cartoonist for The Economist magazine of London and The Baltimore Sun.

In a distinguished career than spans 35 years, Kal has created more than 8,000 cartoons and 140 magazine covers. His resumé includes five other collections of his published work, international honors, awards in seven countries and one-man exhibitions in six.

Since 2006, Kal, a native of Norwalk, CT, has been the Artist-in-Residence at University of Maryland Baltimore County (UMBC). He has created acclaimed animations and calendars, toured the US with Second City, and addressed audiences around the world.

In 1999, The World Encyclopedia of Cartoons said of Kevin "Commanding a masterful style, Kallaugher stands among the premier caricaturists of the (twentieth) century."

Kal lives near Baltimore, Maryland and when not drawing, enjoys snacking on crab cakes and fly fishing in local waters.

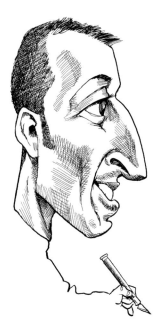

About the Designer

Glenn Dellon

Glenn is the founder and principal of Dellon Design, a multidisciplinary studio specializing in strategy and brand. Founded in 2004, Dellon Design provides creative services across a full spectrum of print, web and environmental graphics.

A native of Baltimore, Glenn attended The Park School and graduated from Tufts University with degrees in Art History and Fine Art. Immediately after college, he earned a graduate certificate in Graphic Design from The Maryland Institute College of Art as well as a Masters degree in Publication Design from the University of Baltimore.

Roughly a zillion years ago during his senior project at Park School, Glenn was an intern for Kal. Since then, the two have stayed in touch and collaborated on some really amazing projects.

These days (relative to the printing of this book), Glenn is into sports birds, cookie butter, and doubles as a pack mule when running errands.

Acknowledgements

The cartoonist and author thanks The Economist for its support throughout the years. In my career with the magazine I have worked at the pleasure of four editors whom I would like to thank: Andrew Knight, Rupert Pennant-Rea, Bill Emmott and John Micklethwait, all of whom have provided me a welcome spot on the Economist team.

Special thanks goes to all my colleagues in The Economist Art Department most notably, department head Penny Garrett and cover designer Graeme James. I am grateful for their patient professional guidance (coupled with a healthy sense of humour) that has made my time with the magazine a pleasure.

I have also worked closely with many other members of staff with special projects. Particular thanks go out to Daniel Franklin, Jane Shaw and Anthony Lopez with The Economist calendars, Justin Hendrix and Dayna DeSimone with Economist events and Ron Diorio with Economist animations.

The author would like to gratefully acknowledge Bill Salganik, who performed the unenviable task as editor of Daggers Drawn, a book written by a chronic mis-speller.

Thanks to Conor Fowler and Stefanie Mavronis for their help creating the video for my Kickstarter project.

Finally, thanks to Glenn Dellon, designer of the book. It has been a great source of pride for me to see my one-time high school intern blossom into a talented and successful professional.